DIFFERENT WAYS OF LOOKING AT GOD

Study by Michael L. Ruffin
Commentary by Judson Edwards

Free downloadable Teaching Guide for this study available at

NextSunday.com/teachingguides

NextSunday Resources
6316 Peake Road
Macon, Georgia 31210-3960
1-800-747-3016
©2021 by NextSunday Resources
All rights reserved.

TABLE OF CONTENTS

Different Ways of Looking at God

HOW TO USE THIS STUDY

NextSunday Resources Adult Bible Studies are designed to help adults study Scripture seriously within the context of the larger Christian tradition and, through that process, find their faith renewed, challenged, and strengthened. We study the Scriptures because we believe they affect our current lives in important ways. Each study contains the following three components:

Study Guide

Each study guide lesson is arranged in four movements:

Reflecting recalls a contemporary story, anecdote, example, or illustration to help us anticipate the session's relevance in our lives.

Studying is centered on giving the biblical material in-depth attention while often surrounding it with helpful insights from theology, ethics, church history, and other areas.

Understanding helps us find relevant connections between our lives and the biblical message.

What About Me? provides brief statements that help unite life issues with the meaning of the biblical text.

Commentary

Each study guide lesson is accompanied by an additional, in-depth commentary on the biblical material. Written by a different author than the study guide, each commentary gives the opportunity for learners to approach the Scripture text from a separate but complementary viewpoint.

Teaching Guide

In addition to the provided study guide and commentary, *NextSunday Resources* also provides a *free* downloadable teaching guide, available at NextSunday.com. Each teaching guide gives the teacher tools for focusing on the content of each study guide lesson through additional commentary and Bible background information. Through teacher helps and teaching options, each teaching guide also provides substance for variety and choice in the preparation of each lesson.

NextSunday
Resources

STUDY INTRODUCTION

Christian faith emphasizes revelation. As believers, we take seriously the fact that we know about God only because God has chosen to reveal God's self to us. When we stop and think about it, it is amazing that God gives any thought to us at all. But it is even more amazing that God wants to enter into relationship with us. Christians believe that God's ultimate revelation to us is in the incarnation. Jesus Christ, who was God with us and the Word made flesh, came as a sign of God's kingdom breaking into the world.

Along the way to Jesus, though, the biblical writers employed many images and metaphors in their attempts to communicate God's revelation. Some of those images are familiar: Father, Shepherd, Judge, and King, for example. In fact, these images are so familiar that we need to revisit them frequently and to ponder their meaning.

In this unit we will examine some less familiar metaphors for God from the Psalms and the Minor Prophets: God as Rock, as Storm, as Fire, and as Beast. Each of these vivid images communicates aspects of God's character. As we understand more about God through this imagery, our relationship with God and our faith in God are strengthened.

These images are not to be taken literally; God is not literally a rock or a storm or a fire or a beast, just as Jesus is not literally a door or a light. Still, we should take the imagery seriously because we want to know God and be known by God. God knows everything about us, although we can never know everything about God. Even so, God has revealed God's self to us in varied ways. All those ways are gifts that we should gladly and enthusiastically receive.

1

ROCK:
GOD AS REFUGE
Psalms 62:5-8; 144-1-4

Central Question
When have I looked to God for safety?

Scripture

Psalms 62:5-8; 144:1-4
Psalm 62:5 For God alone my soul waits in silence, for my hope is from him. 6 He alone is my rock and my salvation, my fortress; I shall not be shaken. 7 On God rests my deliverance and my honor; my mighty rock, my refuge is in God. 8 Trust in him at all times, O people; pour out your heart before him; God is a refuge for us. *Selah*

Psalm 144:1 Blessed be the LORD, my rock, who trains my hands for war, and my fingers for battle; 2 my rock and my fortress, my stronghold and my deliverer, my shield, in whom I take refuge, who subdues the peoples under me. 3 O LORD, what are human beings that you regard them, or mortals that you think of them? 4 They are like a breath; their days are like a passing shadow.

Reflecting
I remember hearing about an interview in which President Jimmy Carter was asked how many times he prayed each day. He replied that he prayed several hundred times a day, going on to explain that he prayed any time something came up for which he needed guidance.

In a presidential debate in Phoenix, Arizona, on October 13, 2004, President George W. Bush said, "My faith plays a big part in my life.... I pray a lot.... And my faith is...very personal. I pray for strength. I pray for wisdom. I pray for our troops in harm's way. I pray for my family. I pray for my little girls."

A recent article on President Barack Obama's "spiritual cabinet" detailed the President's practice of calling several spiritual leaders who join him in prayer over such matters as economic recovery, protection of the military, and wisdom to govern (Burke).

Given the difficulties our leaders face while trying to lead the nation in times when the world is constantly shifting and changing, it comforts us to know that those leaders have the wisdom to turn to the only stable and secure source of help that exists. For refuge and strength, they turn to God, who is the solid rock in any circumstance.

> When has God been your "rock" in trying circumstances?

The events our leaders confront shape our lives and the lives of our families, friends, and fellow church members. We are affected by economic woes, war, and social upheaval. We are also affected by the personal and particular assaults that come in every life to some degree.

Where do we turn when difficulties arise that threaten our stability? Do we turn to things that are less than God? Or do we turn to God who is our refuge and rock? If we turn to God, how do we do so?

Studying

Psalm 62 is a psalm of confidence. In this psalm the writer expresses deep and clear assurance that God is present and dependable for strength and shelter at all times, and especially in times of trouble.

The words in verses 5-6 closely follow those in verses 1-2: "For God alone my soul waits in silence; from him comes my salvation. He alone is my rock and my salvation, my fortress; I shall never be shaken." These opening words of the psalm are a statement of faith. The psalmist affirms that one can wait for God in silence—inner peace—because salvation and deliverance truly come from God alone.

In several places in this psalm the writer repeats a word translated "alone" in the NRSV (vv. 1, 2, 5, 6). In Hebrew this word can also be translated "truly." The repetition of this word drives home the point that God is the only legitimate source of enduring and dependable help.

Both verse 1 and verse 5 state that a person can faithfully wait for God with inner peace. While verse 1 goes on to say, "from him comes my salvation," verse 5 says, "for my hope is from him." When we put the two thoughts together, we see that we can entrust all of life—past, present, and future—to God. Our salvation, our deliverance from whoever and whatever oppresses us, gives us assurance for the present and hope for the future.

The psalmist uses several images in verses 6-7 to describe the God who is the source of salvation and hope. In particular, the words "rock" and "refuge" have extensive histories in the Bible. These words are used as images of God many times in Psalms. For examples we can look at Psalm 61, where the psalmist prays, "Lead me to the rock that is higher than I; for you are my refuge" (vv. 2b-3). There is also the familiar Psalm 46, which affirms that "God is our refuge and strength, a very present help in trouble" (v. 1).

> The Rock, his work is perfect, and all his ways are just. A faithful God, without deceit, just and upright is he....Jacob ate his fill; Jeshurun grew fat, and kicked. You grew fat, bloated, and gorged! He abandoned God who made him, and scoffed at the Rock of his salvation. They made him jealous with strange gods, with abhorrent things they provoked him. They sacrificed to demons, not God, to deities they had never known, to new ones recently arrived, whom your ancestors had not feared. You were unmindful of the Rock that bore you; you forgot the God who gave you birth. (Deut 32:4, 15-18)

The images of "rock" and "refuge" are used in other significant texts in the Old Testament. Extensive use of them is made in the Song of Moses in Deuteronomy 32 and in the Song of David in 2 Samuel 22 (which is repeated in Ps 18). Both songs emphasize the truth that God and God alone is a true, dependable, and faithful rock and refuge.

This imagery is also common in the New Testament. In the concluding words of the Sermon on the Mount, Jesus teaches that those who build their lives on hearing and doing his words are like people who build their houses on a foundation of rock. Again, the ideas of strength and stability are communicated. Jesus himself is called a rock in 1 Corinthians 10:4 and 1 Peter 2:4-8.

These biblical texts and others help us understand the imagery of God as a solid refuge. Beyond this biblical support, our personal experiences testify that God relates to us in this way (Westermann, 152–53). The biblical images become a reality for us as we grow in our trust in God.

Verse 8 marks a change in the psalm. Until now, the focus is on the individual. With verse 8, however, the community of faith comes into view. This verse is an invitation or a summons for those gathered in worship to trust in God for refuge.

We find an interesting contrast between verse 5 and verse 8. Verse 5 expresses the conviction that the trusting person's "soul waits in silence" for God, while verse 8 encourages trusting people to "pour out your heart" before God as an expression of that trust. Pouring out one's heart before God is a valid way to acknowledge the reality of one's trust. Even as we silently wait on God, it is sometimes appropriate for us to cry out to God, to express to God the hard realities of our lives. When we feel the urge to speak to God, we should act on it. We can know with certainty that God hears us.

Psalm 144 is a similar prayer for deliverance in a time of conflict. This psalm praises God for being "my rock and my fortress, my stronghold and my deliverer, my shield, in whom I take refuge" (v. 2). The psalmist also calls God the one "who trains my hands for war, and my finger for battle" (v. 1) and "who subdues the peoples under me" (v. 2).

In this psalm, therefore, the images of "rock" and "refuge," which naturally imply God's defensive help in times of trouble, also have an offensive aspect. God protects us against whomever and whatever would do us harm. At the same time, God also gives us power to be victorious in the world. In other words, the imagery of God as "rock" and "refuge" should not imply a stance of passivity or retreat from the trials of life. On the contrary, through God's help we can also advance triumphantly as we live in the world.

Understanding

What do these two psalms teach us about relying on God in times of trouble? First, while circumstances, events, or people sometimes seem to conspire against us, we can endure if we rely on God.

Believers in Christ are not immune to suffering. Sometimes we deal with troubles that are common to all human beings—illness, financial difficulty, loss of a loved one, broken relationships, and many more. Sometimes our troubles are uniquely related to our Christian faith—doubt, conflict in the church, skepticism from others, and more. We must be careful not to feel as though the world is purposely against us, but it is true that faithful discipleship sometimes provokes opposition from those who reject the lifestyle choices the Bible teaches. Whatever opposition or struggles we face, they are weak and frail compared to God. The Almighty is the solid foundation on which we base our lives. God helps us persevere.

Second, when life becomes hard, we can choose where to turn for help. It is good to cultivate solid character and to develop strong friendships. The fact remains, however, that all human beings fail at times—even those on whom we depend. We rightly lean on our friends and loved ones in difficult times, but we cannot expect them to do the impossible.

In the end, only God is an unshakeable refuge. This doesn't mean we shouldn't work on developing Christian character or finding refuge in a community of faith. It does mean that these sources of comfort work best as conduits for God's perfect and abiding strength.

Third, the images of God as rock and refuge are both defensive and offensive. These verses paint a picture of God as a fortress to which we can retreat in times of trouble. They also call us to remember that God fights our battles and gives us the strength to fight as well. God not only protects us amid the troubles we encounter but also overcomes these troubles in God's own way. The imagery of a rock doesn't mean that God is unmoving. On the contrary, God is a "rock" who goes before us to help us overcome adversity. God sees us through the trouble all the way to the other side.

What About Me?

• *All of us face troubles that threaten our stability and spiritual equilibrium.* The threats may be physical, financial, familial, emotional, or vocational, but whatever their basis they affect our spirits. As Christians, sometimes we struggle to connect with God when the world around us seems to crumble. It can be difficult to nurture a spiritual relationship when we experience trials. How do look for God in unstable times?

• *How can we decide where we will turn in times of crisis before they happen?* It is wise to practice turning to God for refuge even in the good times. This builds our trust in God. We can turn to God daily through regular Bible study, prayer, worship, and Christian fellowship. At the same time, we can practice turning away from invalid sources of strength that experience has shown will let us down.

• *What does it say about our faith if we cry loudly rather than trust peacefully?* Sometimes trusting in God means waiting with inner peace. Sometimes it means pouring out our hearts before the Lord. Either response—or both responses—can be appropriate in a given circumstance.

To trust in God as an unfailing refuge and unwavering rock does not mean our faith will be unfailing or unwavering. We suffer as Christians, but that does not change the fact that we also suffer as human beings. Our reaction to difficulty may reveal both the maturity of our faith and the areas where we still need to grow. Even if we express doubts about God's help, an honest reaction is better than a dishonest one.

Are you currently facing a crisis? How are you responding? How have you responded to crises in the past? What do your responses reveal about your relationship with God?

• *When have you turned to God for strength and stability?* When have you turned elsewhere? What were the results? It is good to learn from both our "successes" and our "failures."

• *As followers of the resurrected Lord Jesus Christ, we know that nothing, not even death, is too great for our God to overcome.* Indeed, the resurrection of Jesus is the greatest indicator that God is our refuge and our rock.

Resources

Daniel Burke, "Obama's spiritual Cabinet shapes policy, tends his soul," *religionnews.com* (9 March 2010) http://www.religionnews.com/index.php?/rnstext/obamas_spiritual_cabinet_shapes_policy_tends_his_soul (Accessed 30 September 2010).

Claus Westermann, *The Living Psalms*, trans. J. R. Porter (Grand Rapids: Eerdmans, 1989).

ROCK:
GOD AS REFUGE
Psalms 62:5-8; 144-1-4

Introduction

The best Christianity always has a "reverent agnosticism" about it. By that, I mean we Christians always need to recognize that our knowledge of God is limited. God is so far above and beyond us that it is simply not honest to pretend we have God figured out.

In Isaiah 55, God, through the prophet, says to the people of Judah, "For my thoughts are not your thoughts, nor are your ways my ways, says the Lord. For as the heavens are higher than the earth, so are my ways higher than your ways and my thoughts than your thoughts" (Isa 55:9-10). The apostle Paul, in his great love chapter, reminds us that we now see "in a mirror dimly, but then we will see face to face. Now I know only in part; then I will know fully, even as I have been fully known" (1 Cor 13:12).

Since God's ways are so much higher than ours, and since we now see only through a mirror dimly, we humans often try to describe our experience of God through metaphors and similes. We can never completely capture the essence of God, but we can try to use these images to explain how God has come to us.

In this unit of study, we will look at four images of God used by people in the Old Testament to depict their experience of the Divine. They said God is like a rock, a storm, a fire, and a beast. As we study these Old Testament images of God, we will not only learn how those ancient people experienced God. We will also get to see if the old images of God are relevant to our experience today.

In this first study, we probe a couple of the psalms that refer to God as "a rock." Quite a few other Old Testament verses use this image (see Deut 32:4, 18, 31; Ps 18:31, 62:6; Isa 26:4), so it was likely a common metaphor among the people of Israel.

What does it mean to describe God as a rock? What facets of God's character were the people of Israel trying to convey? Let's consider two implications of that image.

God Is Eternal

One of the truths they were trying to describe is the eternal nature of God. Everything else will wither and die, but God is the rock that will last forever. As David puts it, "O Lord, what are human beings that you regard them, or mortals that you think of them? They are like a breath; their days are like a passing shadow" (Ps 144:3-4). Humans are like a breath, here one moment and gone the next, but God is the eternal Rock.

That truth must have been a comfort to David, for he knew about the changes that had taken place in the nation of Israel. When he surveyed Israel's history, he saw how uncertain the people's lives had been. He knew about the exodus from Egypt, the wilderness wanderings, the wars with other nations, and the failed reign of King Saul. He knew that political kingdoms come and go and that today's friends can become tomorrow's enemies. David knew there was nothing truly stable in the world.

When he surveyed his personal history, he saw change and uncertainty there, too. He knew from his own experiences that human life is like a passing breath—the death of a baby, the death of a best friend, his tragic sins and their sad consequences, the constant attacks on his character by his "friends." He understood how flimsy and temporary life is. David knew that his own personal kingdom was no sturdier than quicksand.

When David surveyed both his national and personal history, he knew that mortals are like a breath. Their days are like a passing shadow.

But then there is God, the Rock. Though Israel's fortunes rose and fell, God was constant. God was the Rock, the Eternal One, in the midst of all the change. And though David's personal life had been up and down, God was the stabilizing factor. In a topsy-turvy world, it must have been comforting to remember God, the Rock who never changes.

If that was comforting in David's time, it is probably even more comforting in ours. Someone somewhere hit the "fast-forward button" several years ago, and changes are coming at us at a record pace. It is hard to realize that not long ago we knew nothing of cell phones, the Internet, e-mail, or even remote controls. Now, we can't imagine life without those things. I recently read that books, newspapers, and watches can now be considered "endangered species." The old order of things is passing away before our eyes, and all things are becoming new.

Who knows what these changes will mean for our personal lives? Who knows what they will mean for the church and how it will need to minister in the coming days? Who knows the kind of world our children and grandchildren will live in? Who knows if we will be able to survive all the changes that are being forced upon us?

When we think about the dizzy pace of life and the daily changes we face, we can easily start to lose confidence. We can start to have doubts and fears about the future and what it will be like for us and the ones we love. When we were younger, life seemed fairly predictable. But what about now? Who knows what tomorrow might bring?

But then we remember: God is our Rock. In the midst of these exciting and terrifying changes, there is One who is eternal. The same God who created the universe continues to sustain it, now and into the future. God will sustain the universe every day and will sustain us every day. People will come and go, innovations will push us forward, and tomorrow will look different than today, but the Rock will continue to hold our lives together.

When the writer of the book of Hebrews wanted to encourage the early Christians in a world of change and persecution, he told them to remember that "Jesus Christ is the same yesterday and today and forever" (Heb 13:8). That is always a steadying, hopeful word. No matter how fast the world seems to be spinning out of control, God—and the God-Man, Jesus—is eternal.

God Is Dependable

The second truth the biblical writers teach by comparing God to a rock is that God is dependable. God is trustworthy. When you run to the Rock, you will always find it to be a refuge in times of trouble.

David writes in Psalm 62, "For God alone my soul waits in silence, for my hope is from him. He alone is my rock and my salvation, my fortress; I shall not be shaken. On God rests my deliverance and my honor; my mighty rock, my refuge is in God" (Ps 62:5-7).

This is not the only time when David celebrates God as his Rock. In other psalms, he sounds the same note: "The Lord is my rock, my fortress, and my deliverer, my God, my rock in whom I take refuge, my shield, and the horn of my salvation, my stronghold" (Ps 18:2).

It is gratifying to think of God as eternal. It is even more gratifying to think of God as both eternal and a dependable refuge in difficult times. An eternal Rock that consistently provides stability is essential to life.

Everyone has some kind of rock. It is impossible to survive in our hectic world without one. Our rock is whatever gets us out of bed in the morning, whatever gives us meaning, whatever sustains us when the storms of life threaten us. For some, the rock is a person. It may be a husband or wife, a friend, or a child. For some, the rock is a cause: a job, a passion, or a calling.

For some people, the rock is an activity such as coaching baseball, collecting old books, or running marathons. Finally, for some, the rock is something sinister: a drug habit, working around the clock, or dependence on alcohol. Whatever gets us through the day, whatever we depend on for our security, is our rock.

David and some of the other Old Testament saints decided that God would be their rock. They decided they would base their meaning and hope on God: "For God alone my soul awaits in silence, for my hope is from him" (Ps 62:5).

The inescapable truth is that we all have to choose our rocks. We all have to choose who or what gives our lives meaning and hope. It is a personal decision, and a most important one. If we choose to build our lives on a rock that is not eternal or dependable, we might one day discover that we can't survive the storms of life.

Nearly all of the allusions to God as a rock in the Bible are in the Old Testament, but there are some exceptions. The rock image in our two psalms this week brings to mind Jesus' words in the Sermon on the Mount. After spelling out a radically new way of approaching life—a way of complete trust and dependence on God—he concludes by saying,

> Everyone who hears these words of mine and acts on them will be like a wise man who built his house on rock. The rain fell, the floods came, and the winds blew and beat on that house, but it did not fall, because it had been founded on rock. (Matt 7:24-25)

Jesus concludes the Sermon on the Mount by recognizing that we all have to choose the foundation of our lives. We can choose something (or Someone) eternal and dependable, or we can choose something or someone destined to collapse when the storms come. The choice is ours, and the choice is crucial.

Conclusion

We know that the people of the Old Testament often forgot the True Rock. They chased false gods, stumbled into sin, and lived as anything *but* people of God. But they did an interesting thing to try to keep from wandering away from God: they erected rocks to remind themselves of the Rock.

For example, when they finally made it into the promised land after the exodus, they erected twelve stones at a place called Gilgal so they wouldn't forget God. Joshua said to the people, "When your children ask their parents in time to come, 'What do these stones mean?' then you shall let your children know, 'Israel crossed over the Jordan here on dry ground'" (Josh 4:21-22). They set up those stones so they wouldn't forget what God had done for them. The rocks reminded them of the Rock.

Years later, Samuel set up a rock and named it "Ebenezer," which means "stone of help" (1 Sam 7). This reminded the people of the ways God had helped them. That stone was a visual symbol of the True Rock.

This week's lesson launches a new year. As such, it provides the perfect text for considering who or what will be our rock in the twenty-first century. It might be the ideal time to ponder ways God has been our True Rock in the past. As we think about God's faithfulness in years gone by, we will find hope to trust the Rock in this new year.

David said he was going to wait alone in silence and remember his Rock. That would be a wise thing for each of us to do this week: get alone with God and ask him to be our Rock this year.

As we set our course for the coming year, David's question in another psalm is a fine one to ponder: "For who is God except the Lord? And who is a rock besides our God?" (Ps 18:31).

Notes

Notes

2

STORM:
GOD AS CHAOS
Psalm 29

Central Question

How can I trust a God who can't be predicted or controlled?

Scripture

Psalm 29

1 Ascribe to the LORD, O heavenly beings, ascribe to the LORD glory and strength. 2 Ascribe to the LORD the glory of his name; worship the LORD in holy splendor. 3 The voice of the LORD is over the waters; the God of glory thunders, the LORD, over mighty waters. 4 The voice of the LORD is powerful; the voice of the LORD is full of majesty. 5 The voice of the LORD breaks the cedars; the LORD breaks the cedars of Lebanon. 6 He makes Lebanon skip like a calf, and Sirion like a young wild ox. 7 The voice of the LORD flashes forth flames of fire. 8 The voice of the LORD shakes the wilderness; the LORD shakes the wilderness of Kadesh. 9 The voice of the LORD causes the oaks to whirl, and strips the forest bare; and in his temple all say, "Glory!" 10 The LORD sits enthroned over the flood; the LORD sits enthroned as king forever. 11 May the LORD give strength to his people! May the LORD bless his people with peace!

Reflecting

Some of the most memorable baptisms I've conducted involved an element of chaos. There was the boy who, in his rush to get to me so I could baptize him, practically dove into the water, creating rather large waves in the pool. Then there was the lady in her eighties who was terribly afraid of going under water. I leaned her back in the water until every part of her but her face was immersed. At the time I thought she was unnecessarily scared, but the passing years have given me a sense that perhaps she had a healthy appreciation of the chaos the water implied. Maybe we could all learn from her attitude.

Sometimes I wish I could design baptisms so that we could create a sense of chaos—and then a sense of the control of chaos. Imagine if we could churn the waters into a storm as we are being baptized and then have them become calm as we arise out of the water.

Then, perhaps the waters should be stirred up again as we exit the baptistery. That might drive home the lesson that we don't control the experiences of life that follow the baptism. Nor do we control the God who is present in those experiences.

On the Christian calendar, this Sunday is the day to remember the Baptism of our Lord. Psalm 29 is traditionally read on this day. How does our study of the passage help us think about the chaos through which God works in Christ? How does it help us think about the ways God works in and through Christ to control and overthrow the chaos?

Studying

Psalm 29 is a hymn of praise to the Lord. It begins with a summons to praise the Lord (vv. 1-2), moves to a long middle section giving reasons that the Lord should be praised (vv. 3-10), and concludes with a benediction that asks for the Lord to give strength and peace to God's people.

Psalm 29 differs from most hymns of praise in that the summons to praise is directed not to an assembled congregation of worshiping people but to a gathering of "heavenly beings" (v. 1). The Hebrew term here is literally "sons of God." The term is often understood to be a reference to angels.

It is possible that this psalm is an adaptation of a Canaanite song that summoned lesser gods to praise the storm-god Baal. The storm imagery is similar to what is found in known texts that praise the chief Canaanite god. In the hands of the psalmist, however, the imagery describes the power of Yahweh. The psalm envisions the God of Israel presiding over a heavenly court composed of angelic attendants. A similar picture is painted in other biblical passages such as Isaiah 6 and Job 1–2. The passage from Job is especially pertinent because it also mentions the "heavenly beings."

Already in the first two verses, with the depiction of God presiding over a heavenly court of lesser spiritual beings, we catch a glimpse of the magnificent, uncontrollable God. The One who presides over the heavenly court cannot be controlled by the "sons of God," much less domesticated by mere mortals. It is no surprise to learn later in the psalm that this God can come crashing into our world and our lives at will. At the same time, it comes as no surprise that this God who commands the heavenly beings and crashes unexpectedly into our world does so ultimately to bring order to the chaos.

Three times in the opening verses the psalmist uses the word "ascribe" to call upon the heavenly beings to give glory to God. This repetition is a literary device to emphasize the point that the heavenly beings should give God glory. If this is true for heavenly beings, then surely we mortals should do so as well! Indeed, the psalmist offers reasons to glorify the Lord that are visible not only from heaven but also from our vantage point on earth: thunder (v. 3), wind (vv. 5, 8), lightning (v. 7), and earthquakes (v. 8). Although Scripture never asserts that God is a storm, numerous Scripture passages depict a storm accompanying God's approach. The storm can be a sign of God's

Storm imagery is also found in Job 38:1; Psalms 50:3; 97:1-5; Nahum 1:3; and Zechariah 9:14.

holiness (as at Mount Sinai, Exod 19:19) or anger. The danger and unpredictability of a violent storm suggests that there is something dangerous and unpredictable about God.

The psalmist uses the imagery of the chaos of a storm to remind us that, like a storm, God is beyond our control. Just as God is present in the chaos of a storm, God can be present in the chaos that sometimes enters our lives. We should affirm that how and when God comes into our world is not up to us. After

all, even the coming of Jesus was chaotic in many ways. It turned people's expectations completely upside down. But out of the chaos, God worked and still works to bring order.

God in the chaos...God over the chaos...God bringing order to the chaos. It seems familiar, doesn't it? In this passage, we hear echoes of Genesis 1, where the Spirit of God hovers over "the face of the deep," the primeval chaos, and then speaks creation into being. The power of God's word brings order to the chaos.

The echoes are intensified by the sevenfold repetition of the phrase "the voice of the Lord" in verses 3-9. The middle section of the psalm begins by saying that "the voice of the Lord is over the waters; the God of glory thunders, the Lord, over mighty waters" (v. 3). Here, the voice of the Lord—the creating, intervening, acting power of God—moves over the waters. Perhaps we are to imagine the waters of the primeval chaos as in Genesis 1, since the Hebrew word (mayim) is the same. Then, after the sevenfold mention of "the voice of the Lord," we read, "The Lord sits enthroned over the flood" (v. 10). Here the Hebrew word is not mayim but mabbul, the word used for the flood in the story of Noah in Genesis 6–8 (Anderson, 238). This flood involved the breaking loose of the previously contained waters of the primeval chaos (Gen 7:11).

In the Bible, water or flooding is often used as a metaphor for the destructive forces opposed to God's control. For example, Psalm 104 describes God asserting divine sovereignty over creation with respect to "the waters":

> In the beginning when God created the heavens and the earth, the earth was a formless void and darkness covered the face of the deep, while a wind from God swept over the face of the waters. (Gen 1:1-2).

> [T]he waters stood above the mountains. At your rebuke they flee; at the sound of your thunder they take to flight. They rose up to the mountains, ran down to the valleys, to the place that you appointed for them. You set a boundary that they may not pass, so that they might not again cover the earth. (Ps 104:6-9)

The core material of Psalm 29, then, is bracketed on one side by the voice of the Lord over the waters of chaos (v. 3) and on the

other side by the Lord enthroned over the waters of chaos, which always threaten to break loose again (v. 10). Even when God comes in the chaos, God's ultimate purpose is to bring order to it.

Psalm 29 uses another bracketing device in a way that is reflected in a well-known Gospel text. The psalm begins with heavenly beings giving glory to God (vv. 1-2) and ends with a prayer for peace on God's people. The same movement is seen in Luke 2:14, in which the angels proclaim the birth of Jesus to the shepherds (McCann, 164). "Glory to God in the highest heaven" and "peace among those whom he favors" are inseparably connected. Even in the chaos and through the chaos, God is working to bring glory to God and peace for God's people.

> Storms are dangerous, but they are also a blessing. Lightning combines oxygen and nitrogen in the air into a nitrogen compound that is absorbed by the soil. Bacteria in the soil and the roots of plants then transform those nitrogen compounds into different compounds plants need.

Understanding

How does Psalm 29 help us think about trusting in a God who can't be predicted or controlled? First, the writer prompts us to remember that only God knows exactly how God is working out divine purposes. Only God knows the full picture. In this world, we are given a glimpse of the heavenly throne room over which God presides and in which the heavenly beings give God glory. As the psalm progresses, we see that they glorify God for the events evident in creation. There is a larger picture in God's purpose. God is kind enough to give us glimpses of this picture in scriptural imagery.

Second, the writer prompts us to think about God's self-revelation in the world. We might prefer descriptions of the still small voice that Elijah heard (1 Kgs 19:12) or the holy baby in the manger (Lk 2), but Psalm 29 gives us a different picture. This passage turns our thinking toward powerful and even devastating images of God's coming. God does not fit comfortably or willingly into our notions. Perhaps we will better see signs of God's presence and activity as we learn to expand our field of vision.

Third, the writer prompts us to trust that the God who sometimes comes in the chaos will ultimately *overcome* the chaos. The final image in the psalm is of God "enthroned over the flood" and "enthroned as king forever" (v. 10). After that image of enthronement comes a prayer that the Lord will give the people strength and peace. Based on the movement of the psalm, we have every reason to believe that this prayer will be answered.

How God works is up to God. Psalm 29 teaches us that sometimes God works in and through chaos. God's approach is undeniably frightening. But we can have faith that our holy and powerful God is also working to overcome the chaos and bring peace. How this happens is also up to God.

What About Me?

• *How have I limited my ways of thinking about God?* Does this psalm suggest new (though challenging) avenues for me to think about who God is and how God works?

• *How do I think about God in relation to the chaotic events of life?* When chaos comes, some people immediately think, "It is the will of God and so I must accept it." Others think, "God has nothing to do with the chaos because God does not directly cause bad things to happen." Is there a deeper, subtler, and more helpful way to think about the relationship between God and chaos?

• *Is God sometimes a chaotic presence in my life?* Can my faith deepen to the point that I can look for the presence of God directly expressed in events that confuse, confound, and trouble me? Can my faith become courageous and daring? Can my faith welcome an uncontrollable and untamable God rather than timidly settling for a God who fits into easy categories?

• *How can this psalm inform and inspire my perseverance and commitment?* Psalm 29 teaches that we can experience God in the literal and figurative storms of life. It also teaches that God rules over the chaos and will one day completely subdue it. Does the way

God has worked and is working through the death and resurrection of Jesus Christ inform my thinking in this area?

Resources

A. A. Anderson, "Psalms 1-72," *The New Century Bible Commentary* (Grand Rapids: Eerdmans, 1972).

J. Clinton McCann Jr., *A Theological Introduction to the Book of Psalms: The Psalms as Torah* (Nashville: Abingdon, 1993).

Robert Corin Morris, *Wrestling with Grace: A Spirituality for the Rough Edges of Daily Life* (Nashville: Upper Room, 2003).

STORM:
GOD AS CHAOS
Psalm 29

Introduction

Last week's image of God as the True Rock filled us with hope and comfort as we launched a new year. Remembering that God is both eternal and dependable gives us confidence to face the challenges of a new year. Whatever happens, we have built our house on the Rock, and we will be able to withstand the storms that come our way.

This week's image of God is more unsettling. In Psalm 29, David depicts God as a storm, which suggests that God is both mysterious and powerful.

When we deal with God, we are dealing with thunder: "The voice of the Lord is over the waters; the God of glory thunders, the Lord, over mighty waters. The voice of the Lord is powerful; the voice of the Lord is full of majesty" (vv. 3-4).

When we deal with God, we are dealing with lightning: "The voice of the Lord flashes forth like flames of fire" (v. 7).

When we deal with God, we are dealing with a mighty wind: "The voice of the Lord causes the oaks to whirl, and strips the forest bare" (v. 9).

In short, when we deal with God, we are dealing with One who is like a storm: "The Lord sits enthroned over the flood; the Lord sits enthroned as king forever" (v. 10).

Other Old Testament passages also use storm imagery to describe God. Job hears God's voice in a whirlwind (Job 38:1). The psalmist says, "Clouds and darkness are all around him.... His lightnings light up the world; the earth sees and trembles" (Ps 97:2, 4). The prophet Nahum describes God like this:

"His way is in whirlwind and storm, and the clouds are the dust of his feet" (Nah 1:3).

What are those writers trying to tell us about their experience of God? What does this storm imagery convey about God's character and the way God came to the ancient poets and seers?

I think they were trying to tell us at least two things about the nature of God. Like a storm, God is mysterious. And like a storm, God is powerful.

God Is Mysterious

We have a saying here in Texas: if you don't like the weather, just wait a minute. I'm guessing people in Oregon, North Carolina, and Maine say that, too. Everywhere you go, the weather is unpredictable and mysterious.

Though we have sophisticated meteorological instruments that far surpass anything available in Old Testament days, we can still be surprised by a sudden rain or snowstorm. How many times have we said to someone, "I don't think the weatherman saw this storm coming"? Like our Old Testament ancestors, we are at the mercy of wind, rain, heat, and cold and understand that these conditions are beyond both our control and our predictions.

So is God. The Old Testament writers describe God as a storm: mysterious and unpredictable. If we think we have God figured out, we are deluding ourselves. This is obvious when we look at history and at personal experience.

Look first at history. If you had received the chance to predict how God would act throughout history, what would you say? I'm not exactly sure what I would say, but I can tell you for certain what I would *not* say. I would never predict that God would create giraffes, whales, mice, and starfish. I would never predict that God would make orchids, palm trees, grapes, and coffee beans. I would never predict that God would choose to save the world through the tiny nation of Israel. I would never predict that God would come into the world as a baby in a bed of straw. I would never predict that God would want ordinary people, like fishermen and housewives, to establish his kingdom on earth. I would never predict that God would offer people forgiveness through a

Roman crucifixion. I would never predict that God would bring a dead Jesus back to life. I would never predict that God would stay so out of sight or be so low key. And I would never predict that God would give people free choice in loving him or not.

That's not the way any of us would run the universe, but history reveals that's precisely the way God has done it. Truly, God's thoughts are not our thoughts, and our ways are not God's ways. History is bathed in the surprise and mystery of God.

Our personal experience bears the mark of surprise and mystery, too. Honestly, when you look back at the twists and turns in your life, aren't you surprised at what God has done? Aren't you surprised at the ways God has worked?

I could not have anticipated much of what was going to happen to me while I was in the midst of it. Now, as I look into the rearview mirror of my history, I am in awe at the surprising, mysterious ways God has moved. The childhood in Houston. The journey to college and seminary. The marriage to Sherry. The birth of our two children. The two churches I served as pastor during my last thirty-three years in ministry. The books I've written. The people I've come to know. I could not have predicted most of those things, but they now make up my personal story. I look back at everything God has done in my life and feel both surprised and grateful.

Therefore, when we look at history and at our own experience, we can understand what those Old Testament writers meant when they called God a storm. God is mysterious and unpredictable, and the people who trust in God will often be in awe at the surprises God throws at them. As Jesus said to Nicodemus, "The wind blows where it chooses, and you hear the sound of it, but you do not know where it comes from or where it goes. So it is with everyone who is born of the Spirit" (Jn 3:8).

If you hitch your life to God, you'd be wise to buckle your seat belt and get ready for a wild ride.

God Is Powerful

To say God is a storm is also to acknowledge God's power. God is like thunder, lightning, and wind, roaring in power through human history to accomplish divine purposes.

It is interesting to notice the change that takes place in the power of God as Scripture unfolds. In the Old Testament, God's power is straightforward and impressive. God creates the world and all that is in it. God thunders commands from heaven. God parts the waters and defeats Israel's enemies. God is an active storm, showing power in magnificent ways. Martin Luther called this direct, obvious power of God "right-handed power."

But by the time we get to the New Testament, we see a different concept of power. God does dramatic acts like working through Jesus to perform miracles and revealing himself to Saul of Tarsus on the road to Damascus. Once we come to the letters of the New Testament, though, "right-handed power" has given way to "left-handed power." God has chosen to work through unlikely events and people to accomplish his purpose.

Years ago, a writer named Edmund Steimle captured this movement toward "left-handed power" in his book, *From Death to Birth* (Philadelphia: Fortress, 1973). He wrote,

> When God comes to us, he does not overwhelm. He plays it cool. Low key. He always appears to be less than he really is, what someone has called "the ironical man." Like a child born in a stable. Like a young man growing up in a family for years nrecognized for what he really is. Like a prisoner refusing to answer the false accusations of a judge. Like a man riding bareback on a donkey, his heels grabbing the belly of the animal to keep from falling off. God, "the ironical man," always seems to be less than he really is. (71)

Once again, we can probably verify that movement from "right-handed power" to "left-handed power" in our own experience with God. Don't we often wish God would be more obvious in relating to us? Don't we wish for divine thunder and lightning that would give us clear illumination? Don't we long for the storm to blow so loudly in our experience that we know for certain that the God of the universe has just passed by?

But more often than not, we get a quiet, "left-handed power" that makes us wonder if we encountered God at all. Was that God's voice or my own desire? Was that God telling me to do that, or was it simply old patterns of thinking I learned from my childhood? Was that event an expression of God's will or merely some random happening that I have to address? More than we like, our experience mirrors Elijah's in 1 Kings 19 where God did not come to him in the wind, the earthquake, or the fire, but in the mystifying silence.

God still moves. God still displays awesome power. But that power often comes in a silence that both baffles and disappoints us. It comes in quiet, unspectacular ways. And we often comprehend it only when we are attentive to the people and events in our lives.

Conclusion

As I mentioned earlier, this image of God as a storm is not as comforting as the image of God as a rock. To say God is like a storm is to say that God is both mysterious and powerful, which means we can neither understand nor control him.

The God-as-a-storm image actually frustrates us on two fronts. First, it reminds us that we are limited in knowledge and power. God might be like a storm, but we most assuredly are not. We're more like a puddle! We don't really understand what is going on in our world or in our personal experience, and we have little control over what will happen in the future. When we acknowledge that God is a storm, we're also acknowledging that we have no storm-like qualities at all. We have to admit that most days we're in over our heads.

Second, thinking of God as a storm reminds us that the experience of many of the Old Testament writers was different from ours. God has not been as "right-handed" with us as God evidently was with them. One of the frustrations we have with the Bible is precisely at this point. We read Old Testament (and even New Testament) stories about God's lightning and thunder and wonder why we have to settle for silence. The Old Testament image of God-as-a-storm makes us long for a little "storm action" in our own lives.

But the storm imagery still reminds us of something important about the character of God. Because God is like a storm, we dare not pretend to be expert meteorologists in matters relating to God. We dare not presume to know exactly how God will act in our world or even in our own experience. Let's admit it: we don't know how God will end human history, how or when Christ will return, or even what tomorrow will hold for us personally. We truly do see through a glass dimly, and we need to confess that.

But we also need to confess that just because we can't understand or control God doesn't mean God is not alive and well and active. As we saw last week, God is a rock, eternal and dependable, and the world would crumble into nothingness without God's sovereignty. And, as we see in this week's verses, God is a storm, mysterious and powerful, bringing his will to pass on the earth.

Our part is to acknowledge our sin and humanity, to be as honest as we can be, and to love God with all of our heart, mind, soul, and strength. Our part is to trust that even when the storm comes, it comes with winds full of love and grace.

Notes

Notes

3

FIRE:
GOD AS PURIFIER
Malachi 2:17–3:4

Central Question

What does God want to remove from my life?

Scripture

Malachi 2:17–3:4

17 You have wearied the LORD with your words. Yet you say, "How have we wearied him?" By saying, "All who do evil are good in the sight of the LORD, and he delights in them." Or by asking, "Where is the God of justice?" 3:1 See, I am sending my messenger to prepare the way before me, and the Lord whom you seek will suddenly come to his temple. The messenger of the covenant in whom you delight—indeed, he is coming, says the LORD of hosts. 2 But who can endure the day of his coming, and who can stand when he appears? For he is like a refiner's fire and like fullers' soap; 3 he will sit as a refiner and purifier of silver, and he will purify the descendants of Levi and refine them like gold and silver, until they present offerings to the LORD in righteousness.
4 Then the offering of Judah and Jerusalem will be pleasing to the LORD as in the days of old and as in former years.

Reflecting

When I was a college student, I was invited to preach one Sunday night at my home church. As I walked into the sanctuary foyer I was met by a friend of mine who had only recently become serious about his walk with Jesus. With something of a gleam in his eye he asked me, "Are you really going to let us have it tonight?"

I responded, "I'm not good at stepping on people's toes."

The gleam gave way to a look of disappointment as he said, "Well, I hope you're not going to tell us how good we are!"

That conversation clarified an ongoing tension in my faith and in my preaching and teaching. How do we talk about the love and grace of God and the truth that we are God's beloved children while at the same time making it clear that God's love and grace compel God to take our sins seriously? That tension is present in the lives of many Christians; it may be present in yours.

> When have you sensed God "burning away" ungodly aspects of your life? Was this a painful or a pleasant experience? Explain.

We are beloved children of God. If we are to be the children that God wants us to be, what do we need to give over to God so that God can remove it from our lives? How might we benefit from the admittedly painful but needed purification that God wants to bring about in us?

Studying

We know little about the prophet Malachi. Indeed, we may not even know his name! Since "Malachi" means "my messenger," it may be a title or designation rather than a proper name. Nevertheless, it is best to refer to the prophet as Malachi for the sake of tradition and convenience.

In Hebrew tradition, the book of Malachi is the last of the prophetic writings found in the Book of the Twelve. Christian tradition speaks of this collection as the twelve Minor Prophets. In Jewish thinking, the collection became known as the Book of the Twelve because these shorter canonical prophetic writings were put on one scroll. For Christians, these writings came to be known as the Minor Prophets not because their messages are less important but because the collections are simply shorter than those of the Major Prophets Isaiah, Jeremiah, and Ezekiel. Indeed, the message of Malachi is vital in a time like ours—as in any time.

The prophecy of Malachi most likely comes from the mid- to late fifth century BC. This was around 100 years after the initial return from Babylonian exile. In 539 BC, Cyrus of Persia conquered the city of Babylon and took control of the Babylonian empire. In the first year of his reign over Babylon, he issued a decree permitting the exiled Jews to go home (Ezra 1, 6).

The century that followed is called the Restoration Period. During those 100 years the Jerusalem temple was rebuilt in 515 BC. The governors of Judah were Sheshbazzar and Zerubbabel, both of whom had led groups of returnees from Babylon to Judah. The prophets Haggai and Zechariah provided religious leadership. Both of them preached about the restoration of Judah.

Also during this time the wall of Jerusalem was rebuilt under the leadership of the governor, Nehemiah (c. 445 BC). The people also renewed the covenant through the efforts of the priest, Ezra.

Despite these accomplishments, things were not going well in the time of Malachi. In the prophet's view, covenant violations were rampant, and the people needed to be warned of the impending judgment of God. To underscore the seriousness with which God viewed the people's offenses and their inability to comprehend what they were doing, the prophet communicated his message using a particular literary form. This form can be called a dialogue or disputation. Typically, Malachi proposes a statement, either from himself or from God. He follows this statement with a rhetorical question that demonstrates the people's lack of self-awareness. Finally, the prophet gives a response in the name of the Lord. This response usually involves God leveling charges against the people.

When we take this literary device into account, it is clear that our passage properly begins with 2:17, where the prophet says, "You have wearied the Lord with your words."

To this statement the people respond, "How have we wearied him?"

> Through their complaints, the people have tired God. They have asserted that God rewards the evil and that God's justice is absent. Both are such fundamental misunderstandings of God's activity that they deny the possibilities for relationship between God and humans. Belief in God's presence and morality is essential to the faithful life. (Berquist, 801)

The prophet, speaking for God, replies, "By saying, 'All who do evil are good in the sight of the Lord, and he delights in them.' Or by asking, 'Where is the God of justice?'"

The words of the people reveal their mindset. They don't think God has any interest in what they are doing (Achtemeier, 184). The verses that follow (3:1-4) are God's answer. The prophet proclaims that God indeed cares, and that the people will soon see God's care demonstrated.

The Lord says the "messenger of the covenant" will come (3:1). That "messenger of the covenant" is the Lord himself, as the verses that follow make clear. But before the Lord comes, another messenger will come (3:1)—a forerunner.

Our passage leaves that messenger unnamed, and since the Lord can come for judgment—or for any other purpose—at any time, perhaps we should understand that such a forerunner is anyone at any time who proclaims the word of God to prepare the people for God's coming. Even so, later in this book the prophet says, "Lo, I will send you the prophet Elijah before the great and terrible day of the Lord comes" (4:5). The New Testament identifies John the Baptizer as the "Elijah" who paved the way for the coming of the covenant messenger who was Jesus Christ (see Mt 17:10-13).

Still, though John the Baptizer paved the way for the coming of Jesus Christ, and today's preachers of the good news inspire hope in the second coming of Jesus, God's messengers also need to prepare people for the ways God in Christ comes to us for judgment here and now.

The prophet's audience apparently looked forward to the coming of the Lord with great anticipation. Malachi refers to "the messenger of the covenant in whom you delight" (3:1). After two chapters of God's complaints against the people, Malachi's proclamation that God is "sending my messenger to prepare the way before me" was probably not comforting! On the contrary, he portrays the coming of the Lord not as a delight but as an unpleasant and challenging event. "Who can endure the day of his coming," he asks, "and who can stand when he appears?" (3:2).

The prophet uses the imagery of purification. He warns the people that God's coming will be like fire. Fortunately, the prophet has in mind not a blazing wildfire or a devastating explosion but rather a refiner's fire. God's coming, he says, is like a refiner's or smelter's fire and fullers' or launderers' soap. God's purpose is not to destroy but to purify, so that their worship will once again please God.

This is not the only time in scripture where God's holy presence is compared to fire. Isaiah experienced God's purification when an angel touched his tongue with a burning coal from the altar (Isa 6:6-7). Describing a time of future judgment, the author of Hebrews calls God "a consuming fire" (Heb 12:29).

We may take comfort in the idea that the purpose of God's fire is to purify. At the same time, there are other biblical images for purification. Plunging into a cleansing stream or being washed with pure water would surely be a more comforting metaphor! Yet Malachi describes God's cleansing as a fire that burns away our impurities. Sometimes the fire is what we need. Sometimes the work that must be done is so profound that it hurts.

> Fire is also a metaphor of God's presence in Genesis 15:17; Exodus 3:2-4; 13:21; 19:18; Judges 13:20; and 1 Kings 18:24, 38.

God's cleansing and refining activity is especially aimed toward Israel's religious leaders. They need to be cleansed so the worship and service of God's people can be brought up to an appropriate standard (3:3-4).

God's judgment is for everyone's good. Once the people are cleansed and renewed, the prophet says, God will once again

accept their sacrifices. Their reconciliation with God will be complete.

Understanding

God wants to remove harmful attitudes and actions from our lives. How does this passage help us understand that?

First, it teaches that we can develop an ongoing sensitivity to the presence of God in our world and in our lives. Malachi 2:17 exposes the inappropriateness of assuming or presuming that God is not with us—or that if God is with us, God is not interested in us and in what we do. Jesus' incarnation, crucifixion, and resurrection are profound testimony that God is intensely interested in our world and in our lives. Christians must keep Christ in mind when pondering how much God cares about us.

Second, the passage challenges us to become aware of the messengers God sends to warn us of God's judgment. Malachi expected a messenger who would prepare the way for the Lord to come in judgment. The Gospels see John the Baptizer as such a messenger. Which messengers sound appropriate words of warning today? Which ones sound inappropriate warnings? Do these messengers strike a healthy balance between God's justice and God's grace and love? Do they display humility about their convictions? After all, even John the Baptizer, who comes across as dogmatic in his preaching, later asked Jesus, "Are you the One?" Do the messengers to whom we listen display an awareness that they too need to experience God's cleansing fire, as did the priests of Malachi's day?

Third, the passage challenges us to become sensitive to attitudes and actions that God wants to remove from our lives. God wants to shape us into followers of Jesus Christ who are always growing. Scripture, prayer, and involvement in Christian community reveal the places in us that need cleansing or refining. Such spiritual practices also improve our willingness to submit to such cleansing and refining.

What About Me?

• *How does the Lord come to us?* We have recently come out of the Advent and Christmas seasons, during which we often hear about the first and second comings of Jesus. We must never stop looking back on Jesus' birth or forward to his return. Nevertheless, we live in the here and now. The Lord also comes to us in the present. God comes to comfort and strengthen us but also to challenge and change us. Do we look for the comfort but not for the challenge?

• *What needs to change for us to be more fully the people God wants us to be?* Some people make the mistake of living as if how they think or what they do makes no difference to God. Others make the mistake of living as if nothing they think or do is good enough for God. Either extreme can lead to spiritual and ethical paralysis. The truth is that we are all a mixed bag. We have characteristics God commends and ones that God condemns. To make spiritual progress, we must sometimes focus on what is wrong in us so that we can receive God's conviction and forgiveness. Then we will be able to live in light of what God has done in us.

• *How have we experienced the purifying power of God?* Can you name past experiences that you now see as the painful process of God's purification or refinement? How have these experiences led you to be more completely the person you were meant to be?

Resource

Elizabeth Achtemeier, "Nahum–Malachi," *Interpretation* (Atlanta: John Knox, 1986).

John L. Berquist, "Malachi," *Mercer Commentary on the Bible*, ed. Watson E. Mills et al. (Macon GA: Mercer University Press, 1995).

FIRE:
GOD AS PURIFIER
Malachi 2:17–3:4

Introduction

We have come to our third Old Testament image in this unit
on "Different Ways of Looking at God." This week we look at a
passage in Malachi where the prophet alludes to God as a fire:
"For he is like a refiner's fire and like fullers' soap; he will sit as a
refiner and purifier of silver, and he will purify the descendants
of Levi and refine them like gold and silver, until they present
offerings to the Lord in righteousness" (Mal 3:2-3).

To understand this allusion to God as a refiner's fire, we have
to go back to the first two chapters in Malachi to see what needed
to be refined. The people of Judah were guilty of at least four sins
that the prophet spells out in those first two chapters.

First, the people were limiting God by assuming that God
was only concerned about Judah: "For from the rising of the
sun to its setting my name is great among the nations, and in
every place incense is offered to my name, and a pure offering;
for my name is great among the nations, says the Lord of hosts"
(1:11). God's name was great among the nations, but the people
of Judah assumed God was focused only on them. They needed a
bigger God.

Second, the people were giving God less than their best:
"You bring what has been taken by violence or is lame or sick,
and this you bring as your offering" (1:13). Malachi told them
that God deserved better.

Third, the priests were faithless and evil: "But you have
turned aside from the way; you have caused many to stumble by
your instruction; you have corrupted the covenant of Levi, says

the Lord of hosts" (2:8). The religious leaders needed to repent so the people could get a clear understanding of God.

Fourth, both the priests and the people had divorced the true God and married false gods: "Judah has been faithless, and abomination has been committed in Israel and in Jerusalem; for Judah has profaned the sanctuary of the Lord, which he loves, and has married the daughter of a foreign god" (2:11). Everyone was following after false gods, and the true God was being ignored.

But, the prophet warns, the God of fire is coming to refine Judah and make it pure. Once that fire has consumed the people, "then the offering of Judah and Jerusalem will be pleasing to the Lord as in the days of old and as in former years" (3:4).

So what does the imagery of God as a fire tell us about God? When the writer of the book of Hebrews declares that "our God is a consuming fire" (Heb 12:29), what does he mean?

Let's consider two possible meanings of this fire imagery. First, God-as-fire teaches us that God is *active*, both in history and in our individual lives. Second, God-as-fire teaches us that God is confrontational, sweeping into the inner recesses of our souls to make us pure.

God Is Active

Part of the meaning of the fire imagery is so obvious we're prone to overlook it. When Malachi says that God is like a refiner's fire, he is implying that God is active. Like a fire, God blazes into our lives to make a difference, to burn out sin and purify our hearts. The fire imagery reminds us that God is personal and active.

Perhaps we can see that more clearly if we think of a couple of other images the prophet could have used to describe God.

He could have said that God is a *dream*, implying that God doesn't actually exist. God might be a dream that we humans have created to give us strength in life and hope in death. Certainly, many in our day hold to this image of God-as-dream and believe that God doesn't exist at all. God is manmade, they say, and wise people have cast off this old philosophy to live boldly without an illusion of deity.

Or the prophet could have said that God is a *statue*, implying that God exists but doesn't do anything. God stands still as stone, feeling no compassion and lifting not even one finger to help. God is the Unmoved Mover who started the whole process and then withdrew into seclusion. If God is a statue, it is foolish to think of him in personal terms or to come to him in prayer.

But, according to Malachi, God is not a dream or a statue. God is a *fire*. And if God is a fire, God has passion. A fiery God cares, relates, and, as we will see in a moment, confronts. Malachi's God is alive and well and concerned about the people of Judah.

In the Old Testament we hear about God's activity primarily as it relates to the nation of Israel and, eventually, the southern kingdom of Judah. In the Old Testament, God is concerned about a nation. Then, in the New Testament, God's activity shifts toward individual people. One of the great contributions of Jesus to our understanding of God is precisely at this point. Jesus made it clear that God is concerned about individual people, that the divine fire is not just aimed at a nation but at individuals.

According to Jesus, we should pray to God as "Abba," a term of endearment and trust. God is a loving Father we can approach with confidence and trust. According to Jesus, God knows the number of hairs on our heads. We are not lost in the mass of humanity; we are known and loved individually. Jesus took God's grace and love and pointed them directly at you and me. Each of us is of worth to God, and each of us can have the fire of God in our lives.

The fire of God is not only raging in the world; it is raging in each of our respective hearts. God is not just active in human history; God is active in *my* history and *your* history.

God Is Confrontational

This activity of God includes his willingness to confront us when we go astray. When Malachi describes God as a refiner's fire, he is saying that God confronts the people of Judah about their sins. God cares enough about them to try to guide them to repentance. For their own good, they need to have the fire of God burn in their midst.

Occasionally, when you drive the freeways of Texas in the summer you see a shocking sight. A fire rages on the grassy median beside the freeway. At first you're startled and afraid, but then you notice that men are watching the fire and carefully controlling it. The Texas Highway Department has determined that one way to prevent grass fires in a time of drought is to do a "preemptive burn." Highway workers intentionally set fire to parts of the grassy median so that if someone tosses a cigarette onto the side of the road and a fire ignites, it can only burn so far. Once that fire reaches the already burned area, it has no place to go. The fire goes out.

That might be a good way to think of the fire of God in our lives. God cares enough about us to want to do a preemptive burn in our souls. He confronts us with our sin so that we can recognize and deal with it. If we acknowledge it quickly enough, it will burn out before it causes major damage. Left unchecked, though, that sin will destroy our marriage, family, health, or sanity. Without the confronting fire of God in our lives, the fire of sin can burn forever and destroy us.

When Malachi talks about the fire of God as refining and purifying us, he is describing one of the primary ways God changes us. God changes us by burning away all that is not essential. Just as fire burns away all that is not pure in gold or silver, so God burns away all that is not necessary in our lives.

Our culture lives by the motto, "more is better." We automatically assume that more money is better than less money, more house is better than less house, more activity is better than less activity, and so on. In fact, we devote our whole lives to getting "more."

Then the fire of God starts raging through our souls, and when that fire comes it doesn't add. It subtracts. It makes us look long and hard at what we have and do and asks us a disturbing question: Is this really essential? The fire of God preaches a counter-cultural sermon we would rather not hear: "But strive first for the kingdom of God and his righteousness, and all these things will be given to you as well" (Mt 6:33).

When we experience the fire of God, the chances are good that we will have to get rid of some things. Just as the people of Judah needed to get rid of their limited concept of God, their spiritual lethargy, their evil priests, and their foreign gods, so, too, will we have to part with some nonessentials. The materialism has to go. So must the lust that is wreaking havoc on our marriages. The dishonest religion that makes us hypocrites. The crowded calendar that is killing our family lives. And on and on it goes. The list of sinful nonessentials is unique to each of us, but when the fire of God illumines our minds, we see those nonessentials clearly, and we know they are doing us harm. Though it hurts to see those things go, we know they will destroy us if left unchecked.

God is trying to save us by doing a preemptive burn. God illumines our minds and stirs our consciences so that we will make the necessary changes and become whole again. Then, like Malachi hoped would happen to the people of Judah, the offering of our lives will once again be pleasing to God.

Conclusion

While I was writing this lesson, fire fell from heaven. Yesterday afternoon, in the midst of a rainstorm, lightning struck a tree outside our house and sent a huge limb crashing onto our roof. Fortunately, only a little guttering was damaged.

This event was a stark and ironic reminder of the power of fire. One bolt of lightning sent a giant limb crashing onto our house. I was reminded of the words of James in his discourse on the power of the tongue: "How great a forest is set ablaze by a small fire!" (Jas 3:5). We are grateful that one bolt of fire didn't destroy our whole house.

The fire of God usually strikes our lives in small, unexpected ways. We read a book. We meet a person on the street. We notice the evil in someone else. We do something awful that shows us how evil we are. Or we read a verse of Scripture that hits us right where we live. These are all seemingly little things, but those little bolts of fire strike a responsive chord within us and end up being the very fire of God that prompts us to change.

We can only hope that the little book of Malachi was a lightning bolt for the people of Judah. We hope that they heard the prophet's words, owned up to their sin, and made the necessary changes.

We can only hope and pray that the fire of God will continue to strike us. We should always be grateful that God is active enough to confront us when we're headed in the wrong direction.

And, from time to time, we should probably say a prayer that goes something like this: "Thank you, God, that you are not a mere dream or a stoic statue. Thank you for caring enough about me to be a refiner's fire."

Notes

Notes

4

BEAST:
GOD AS AVENGER
Hosea 13:4-8

Central Question

What makes God angry?

Scripture

Hosea 13:4-8

4 Yet I have been the LORD your God ever since the land of Egypt; you know no God but me, and besides me there is no savior. 5 It was I who fed you in the wilderness, in the land of drought. 6 When I fed them, they were satisfied; they were satisfied, and their heart was proud; therefore they forgot me. 7 So I will become like a lion to them, like a leopard I will lurk beside the way. 8 I will fall upon them like a bear robbed of her cubs, and will tear open the covering of their heart; there I will devour them like a lion, as a wild animal would mangle them.

Reflecting

In January 2010 a devastating earthquake struck the island nation of Haiti. From a geological perspective, the earthquake was caused by the release of stress that had built up along the fault line between two tectonic plates beneath Haiti. Some Christian leaders with a public platform, however, connected the earthquake to a supposed deal with the devil that some Haitians had made through a voodoo ritual during Haiti's struggle for independence from France some two centuries ago. Haiti, their logic went, had been under a curse from God ever since, and this earthquake might be further evidence of it.

Other Christians pointed out the flaws in such reasoning, including the fact that we have to take Jesus into account. In John 9, we read,

> As he walked along, he saw a man blind from birth. His disciples asked him, "Rabbi, who sinned, this man or his parents, that he was born blind?" Jesus answered, "Neither this man nor his parents sinned; he was born blind so that God's works might be revealed in him." (Jn 9:1-3)

Jesus said that questions of fault or blame are inappropriate. What matters, as Jesus goes on to say, is that we who follow him serve as channels of God's grace, mercy, and love in the situations people face.

On the other hand, Jesus also said,

> Those eighteen who were killed when the tower of Siloam fell on them—do you think that they were worse offenders than all the others living in Jerusalem? No, I tell you; but unless you repent, you will all perish just as they did. (Lk 13:4-5)

Jesus said we need to take our sins seriously and understand that there can be ramifications for them.

Some Christians seem to think and live as if nothing makes God angry. Others seem to think and live as if everything does. Can we make God angry? How? And what does God do with such anger?

Studying

Along with Amos, Isaiah, and Micah, Hosea was one of the great eighth-century BC biblical prophets. Hosea is unique among the so-called "writing prophets"—the prophets who have biblical books named after them—in that he was the only native of the northern kingdom of Israel who also preached primarily to that kingdom. (Amos preached to Israel but was a native of the southern kingdom, Judah.) Thus, Hosea's words of judgment against Israel are close to home. He symbolically lived out the tragic relationship between God and Israel in his own relationship with his wife, Gomer (see Hos 1–3).

Hosea's ministry most likely began during the later years of the reign of King Jeroboam II of Israel (who died c. 746 BC) and continued until sometime near the time of Israel's conquest by the Assyrians and the fall of its capital, Samaria, around 723 BC.

From a political and economic point of view, the reign of Jeroboam II had been successful. By contrast, the years between the end of his reign and the fall of Samaria were characterized by instability and decline. This generation saw a succession of six kings with short and ineffective reigns. At the same time, King Tiglath-Pileser III of Assyria enjoyed a long and effective reign (745–27 BC) and succeeded in keeping Israel—and indeed all of the surrounding nations—under his thumb. Finally, as a result of a fool-hardy rebellion, Tiglath's successors Shalmaneser V and Sargon II brought the northern kingdom to an end.

The Last Kings of Israel
(According to William F. Albright, cited by Christensen, 149)

746–45	Zechariah
745	Shallum
745–38	Menahem
738–37	Pekahiah
737–32	Pekah
732–24	Hoshea

Especially when seen in the context of the chapter and the entire book, Hosea 13:4-8 offers a succinct summary of Israel's history from God's perspective. But why did this history unfold as it did? Hosea 13:1-3 describes how the Israelites corrupted their religion by combining the worship of God with the worship of the Baals, local Canaanite deities. This was the primary symptom of Israel's sin of violating their covenant with the God of their ancestors.

This apostasy began centuries earlier, when Jeroboam I, the first king of the northern kingdom, rejected the Jerusalem temple and established rival sanctuaries at Dan and Bethel (1 Kgs 12:28-32). In each sanctuary he set up golden calves and announced to the people, "You have gone up to Jerusalem long enough. Here are your gods, O Israel, who brought you up out of the land of Egypt" (2 Kgs 12:28). This explains Hosea's stunning Accusation in 13:2: "People are kissing calves!" (v.2).

In verses 4-6, Hosea describes God's faithfulness to Israel in terms of a shepherd tending to his sheep. Indeed, the verb "fed" in verse 6 can be translated "pastured" (Mays, 173). Hosea uses that language to explain the basis for God's exclusive claim on Israel. It was God who brought Israel out of Egypt and it was God who had taken care of them ever since (v. 4). It was God alone who was known as God to them, and God alone was their Savior (v. 4). It was God who took care of them in the wilderness before they entered the land of promise (v. 5).

From the standpoint of Israel's history, verse 6 is a kind of bridge. Previously, God had "pastured" the people in the wilderness and later in the promised land. But they sinned both in the wilderness and in the land by forgetting that God had taken care of them. Self-centeredness fueled this forgetfulness. The final result of Israel's self-centeredness was a sense that the most important thing in their lives was their own satisfaction. They came to believe this was something for which they could give themselves—or their false gods—the credit. Mays explains,

> That Israel thought their own satisfaction exhausted Yahweh's purpose, that his acts led to their self-exaltation in pride against him, was bitterest frustration—and out of that bitterness the vehemence of the following sentences (vv. 7f.) unfolds (175).

Hosea employs graphic language in his description of God's anger at Israel's sin (vv. 7-8); God will be "like a lion" and "like a leopard" (v. 7), and God will "fall upon them like a bear robbed of her cubs" (v. 8).

This last phrase is especially suggestive since God's "cubs"— God's children—were the people of Israel. Perhaps Hosea is suggesting that the reason for God's fierce intervention is that God's children are in danger. We see here a protective side of God. God lashes out, but only because God's children are endangered in some way. Ironically, however, God's children had put themselves in danger, and therefore the divine "mother bear" threatens to act against those children. God gets angry when we forget God's benefits, and God's discipline is for our own sake, even when it seems harsh.

Having broken covenant with God, Israel now faces fierce and frightening divine judgment. We find similar imagery in Isaiah 31:4, where God is described as coming down to fight like a lion growling over its prey. Elsewhere, Amos compares the voice of God to the voice of a lion (Amos 3:8).

What does it mean to imagine God as a fierce, ravenous beast? At the very least, it is an image of divine anger or wrath. The biblical writers are clear, however, that this wrath has a purpose. When we take the entire book of Hosea into account, we are led to consider the redemptive and constructive purposes of God's anger. For example, consider Hosea 11, a passage that contains many of the same themes as today's text. After describing God's saving activity on behalf of Israel, God's says that Israel will be ravaged, consumed, and devoured because of their apostasy (11:6). But then God says, "How can I give you up, Ephraim? How can I hand you over, O Israel? ...I will not again destroy Ephraim; for I am God and no mortal" (11:8-9).

In similar fashion, the devastating language of chapter 13 is followed by language of reclamation and redemption in chapter 14. God's anger has a redemptive purpose.

Understanding

How does this text help us think about God's anger? First, it tells us that God's anger must be taken seriously. The language that compares God to a lion, a leopard, and a mother bear strikes us as exaggerated. It is symbolic, but we should take its intensity seriously. God judges sin. God, who is holy, will not take being sinned against lightly. In particular, according to Hosea, God takes it seriously when God's people fail to appreciate the depth of God's love and care for them.

Second, God's anger results from God's intimate involvement in our lives. Drawing on the observations of Abraham Heschel on the suffering of God, Walter Brueggemann said,

> The particular focus of Heschel on God's hurt in the traditions of Hosea and Jeremiah makes abundantly clear that the God of Israel is unlike the God of any scholastic theology and unlike any of the forces imagined in any of the vague spiritualities

available among us. The peculiar character of this God is as available agent who is not only able to act but is available to be acted upon. (9)

We gain a better perspective on the use of animal imagery to describe God's avenging work when we think about the personal involvement of Israel's God with Israel and, by implication, with believers today.

Perhaps the only way to have a God who does not get angry enough to take drastic action against sin is to have a God who is not intimately and personally involved with us. And what kind of "God" would such a "God" be? Certainly not a God who worked through incarnation, crucifixion, and resurrection.

Third, God's anger is ultimately redemptive in purpose. According to Hosea, even as God passed judgment on Israel, God never abandoned hope that the people would repent so that they could be blessed. God avenges himself not for the sake of vengeance but for the sake of reconciliation.

> **?** How is God's capacity to feel hurt or insult related to God's capacity to love?

What About Me?

• *What do we need to remember about what God has done for us?* What can we do to make sure we never forget? God was angry because the people of Israel had for so long forgotten what God had done for them in the exodus, the wilderness, and the promised land. Do we forget what God has done for us in Christ? How can we be sure to remember?

• *Are there sins in my life or in the life of my community that are like the sins of Israel in Hosea's day?* Israel's sins involved forgetting all that God had done for them and mixing their allegiance to God with allegiance to the gods prevalent in their culture. Are we guilty of such sins now? How so?

• *Can and should we share in the anger of God?* If so, how? This is dangerous territory because, while God's anger comes from God's commitment, grace, and holiness, we have to work hard to keep our anger from coming from our ego, pride, and self-centeredness. And yet, Jesus cleansed the temple (Mk 11:15-16), and we are now the body of Christ in the world. What kinds of actions can and should we take? What safeguards can help us ensure that our anger is genuinely an expression of God's anger?

Resources

Walter Brueggemann, *An Unsettling God: The Heart of the Hebrew Bible* (Minneapolis: Fortress, 2009).

Duane L. Christensen, "Chronology," *Mercer Dictionary of the Bible*, ed. Watson E. Mills et al. (Macon GA: Mercer University Press, 1990).

C. S. Lewis, *The Lion, the Witch, and the Wardrobe* (New York: Harper Collins, 1994).

James Luther Mays, "Hosea," *The Old Testament Library* (Philadelphia: Westminster, 1969).

BEAST:
GOD AS AVENGER
Hosea 13:4-8

Introduction

Last week, we considered the image of God as a fire. We saw that the image implies at least two things about God: God is active and God is confrontational. The fire of God burns in our lives to refine us and lead us to renewal.

This week's image, God as a beast, takes those thoughts a step further. Hosea likens God to a lion, a leopard, and a bear. In the process, he implies that God will take drastic measures to ensure our faithfulness. To say that God is like a fire and both active and confrontational doesn't quite capture the intensity of God's character. We must also say that God will go to extreme lengths to draw us to him.

Hosea uses animal imagery to describe the catastrophe about to come upon Israel. In a few short decades, the Assyrians will conquer them and haul them into captivity. In effect, Hosea's prophetic word was, "Get ready, Israel. God is going to use Assyria to tear open the covering of your heart, devour you like a lion, and mangle your dreams." It was not a pretty picture, but Hosea's prophecy came true. In 722 BC, the Assyrians conquered Israel.

The image of God as a beast says that God can and will take drastic measures to bring us closer to him. God's love is so extreme that it will even lead us to some kind of death—the death of a dream, a job, a church, a relationship—so that we can have a resurrection on the other side.

As awful as our focal passage seems, the notion of God as avenger gives way to the image of God as redeemer. In the next chapter, Hosea has God say about Israel, "I will heal their disloyalty; I will love them freely, for my anger has turned from them.... They shall live again beneath my shadow, they shall flourish as a garden; they shall blossom like the vine, their fragrance shall be like the wine of Lebanon" (Hos 14:4, 7).

The book of Hosea promises that if God ever looks like the beast of death to us, it is only because he wants to lead us to resurrection. Something must die so that something new can blossom.

Let's consider two implications of Hosea's image of God as a beast. First, it implies that God is dangerous. Second, it implies that God is relentless.

God Is Dangerous

It is always tempting to picture God as the benevolent Man Upstairs, tottering onto the celestial veranda each morning to check on the world. Then the Man Upstairs retires to his bedroom for a day of divine rest and relaxation.

If we're ever tempted to picture God that way, a quick reading of Hosea 13 will put a different picture in our minds. According to Hosea, God is an angry bear robbed of her cubs, a devouring lion on a rampage, and a manic wild animal mangling everything in its path. Hosea pictures God as a dangerous beast not to be treated casually.

We took our little grandsons to the zoo not long ago and, of course, had to issue the requisite warnings: Don't get too close to the cages. Don't touch any of the animals. Don't make any noises that will disturb the animals. Don't do anything, in other words, to rile these sleeping beasts. Please, grandsons, let's let all of these sleeping tigers lie and get home in one piece.

In her book, *Teaching a Stone to Talk* (New York: Harper & Row, 1982), Annie Dillard suggests we ought to issue similar warnings to people who come to church:

> On the whole, I do not find Christians, outside of the catacombs, sufficiently sensible of conditions. Does anyone have the foggiest what sort of power we so blithely invoke? Or, as I suspect, does no one believe a word of it? The churches are children playing on the floor with chemistry sets, mixing up a

batch of TNT to kill a Sunday morning. It is madness to wear
ladies' straw hats and velvet hats to church; we should all be
wearing crash helmets. Ushers should issue life preservers and
signal flares; they should lash us to our pews. For the sleeping
god may wake someday and take offense, or the waking god may
draw us out to where we can never return. (82)

The prophet Hosea was telling Israel that God had awakened
and taken offense and that they would do well to put on their
crash helmets. But we know that God is dangerous not only
because of prophets like Hosea; we also know God is dangerous
because of who Jesus was. Jesus, God incarnate, revealed God to
be anything but the benevolent Man Upstairs.

Here's the way Thomas Howard describes Jesus in his book,
Christ the Tiger (Philadelphia: Lippincott, 1967):

What he spoke, he spoke loudly and freely, and his words were
their own defense.... Try as we might, we could not own him.
We could not protect him. We could not incarcerate him. For he
always emerged as our judge, exposing our cynicism and fright
by the candor and boldness of his love. He tore our secularist
schemes to ribbons by announcing doom and our religious
schemes to tatters by announcing love. (128)

Long before Christ the Tiger entered history to show how
dangerous God is, Hosea announced that truth to the people of
Israel. God is a leopard, a bear, and a lion, he said, coming among
us to enact judgment.

God Is Relentless

The beast images in Hosea also tell us that God is relentless.
A bear that has been robbed of her cubs will wreak havoc to get
those cubs back. That is the way God is. Like that bear—and like
the lion and leopard Hosea mentions—God will be relentless in
pursuing us.

In his poem "The Hound of Heaven," Francis Thompson
describes his flight from God. He is a man running through the
labyrinth of life, trying to escape God. But God will not let him

be. God is the Hound of Heaven, pursuing him through all of those labyrinths, desperate to find him and love him.

That Hound of Heaven image gives us an accurate way to summarize the biblical story. From beginning to end in Scripture, God is the Hound of Heaven, relentless in pursuit of humanity.

The Bible begins with the story of Adam and Eve and God's willingness to seek them even after they have sinned. Then, throughout the rest of the biblical drama, God keeps pursuing people. He seeks Noah, the drunk; Moses, the murderer; Jacob, the swindler; David, the adulterer; Hosea, the jilted lover; Amos, the country bumpkin; Rahab, the prostitute; Sarah, the skeptic; and Jonah, the reluctant doubter. The Old Testament is filled with the theme of the Hound of Heaven, as God chases down ordinary, sinful people and vows to love and use them.

That theme continues even stronger in the New Testament. Jesus comes into the world declaring that he will seek and save those who are lost. It's as if he is on a divine rescue mission, scouring the highways and hedges for people who need forgiveness and love. Gradually he reels them in: Peter, James, John, Zacchaeus, the woman at the well, the woman caught in the act of adultery, and the angry Pharisee named Saul of Tarsus. He seeks them all and saves them all because that is what he came to do.

And he tells stories about God's relentless love. He says that God is like a shepherd who loses one sheep and cannot sleep until he has found that sheep and brought it safely home. So he searches and searches until he finds it, then puts that sheep on his shoulders, carries it home, and has a party.

Jesus says that God is like a woman who loses a coin, and it drives her crazy. So she lights a lamp, furiously sweeps the house until she finds it, and then calls her friends and neighbors to rejoice with her.

He says that God is like a father who loses a son, and it breaks his heart. So he stands on the porch day after day, hoping the son will return, and, when he finally does, the father kills the fatted calf, puts a ring on the boy's finger and sandals on his feet, and invites everyone to celebrate.

Those three stories in Luke 15 all carry the same message: God's love is relentless. He is willing to work, search, and wait to ensure that we get found. I know it seems like a stretch to tie the awful images in Hosea—wild animals destroying Israel—to those stories of grace in Luke. But they stem from the same divine impulse. They both teach that God is relentless in his pursuit of people. God will do anything—even use the wicked Assyrians—to restore a right relationship with humanity.

What Hosea 13 does, among other things, is remind us that God is not neutral about us. God wasn't neutral about Israel, and God is not neutral about us. God *cares*. God is passionate about us. Even when God throws what seems like a divine temper tantrum, it is actually more like a mother disciplining her child for running into the street. God's anger is a direct result of God's caring. If God didn't care, God could leave us alone. But since God does care, God is a mother bear willing to do anything to assure the safe return of her beloved babies.

Brennan Manning once wrote a book with an odd title: *The Furious Longing of God.* It seems like a strange coupling of words. "Furious" and "longing" don't usually go together. But that title captures not only a vital aspect of God's character but also Hosea's point in our passage. God has a furious longing that we stay in right relationship to him.

Conclusion

Let's be honest: Hosea 13:4-8 is not the kind of passage we would naturally read for our morning devotional. It paints God as violent and judgmental. Who wants to read about a God who is a beast? But beneath the beast imagery are two important truths about God. First, God is dangerous, and we would be wise not to be too flippant or casual as we relate to him. Second, God is relentless, and we can at least appreciate the fact that a beast is neither apathetic nor afraid. God, the beast, will find us at all costs.

For four weeks we've explored some Old Testament images of God: Rock, Storm, Fire, and Beast. We have considered the meaning of those images and have probed eight possible characteristics of God they suggest: God is eternal, dependable, mysterious, powerful, active, confrontational, dangerous, and relentless.

Even as we have piled up our adjectives about God, we know that we could come up with eight more adjectives about God next month. God is inexhaustible, and studying God is like trying to capture the ocean in a teacup. We tiptoe to the edge of the ocean and dip our cups in the water, but we know there is more there than our little cups can possibly hold.

Thankfully, we have enough in our cups to build a life of hope, meaning, and joy. Those Old Testament images of God help us, but the coming of Jesus into the world has helped us even more. As John put it, "No one has ever seen God. It is God the only Son, who is close to the Father's heart, who has made him known" (Jn 1:18).

If nothing else, our four studies of Old Testament images for God have probably given us a greater appreciation for Jesus. The thought of God as Rock, Storm, Fire, and Beast fills us with insight, but the thought of God as Savior fills us with joy.

Notes

Notes

www.ingramcontent.com/pod-product-compliance
Lightning Source LLC
Chambersburg PA
CBHW060708030426
42337CB00017B/2800